SHARK QUEST

Written by Emily Kington

CONTENTS

First published in 2024 by
Hungry Tomato Ltd
F15, Old Bakery Studios,
Blewetts Wharf, Malpas Road,
Truro, Cornwall,
TR1 1QH, UK.

Thanks to our editor, Julie Tofflemire.

A CIP catalog record for this book is available from the British Library.

ISBN 9781835690185
Manufactured in the USA

Discover more at
www.hungrytomato.com

All words in **BOLD** can be found in the glossary.

POWERFUL PREDATORS!

Sharks are among the fiercest and toughest **predators** in the ocean. When they're on the hunt, their **prey** doesn't stand a chance.

YOU DON'T WANT TO MESS WITH SHARKS!

OLDER THAN DINOSAURS

**Sharks have been around for a long time...
over 400 million years!**

These amazing creatures were ruling the seas even before dinosaurs existed – about 190 million years earlier!

Most of a shark's body is made of **cartilage**, so we don't have full **fossils** of them. However, there are plenty of shark teeth fossils.

GREAT WHITES ARE HUGE, BUT MEGALODONS WERE EVEN BIGGER!

It's no surprise that we find shark teeth because there are so many of them!

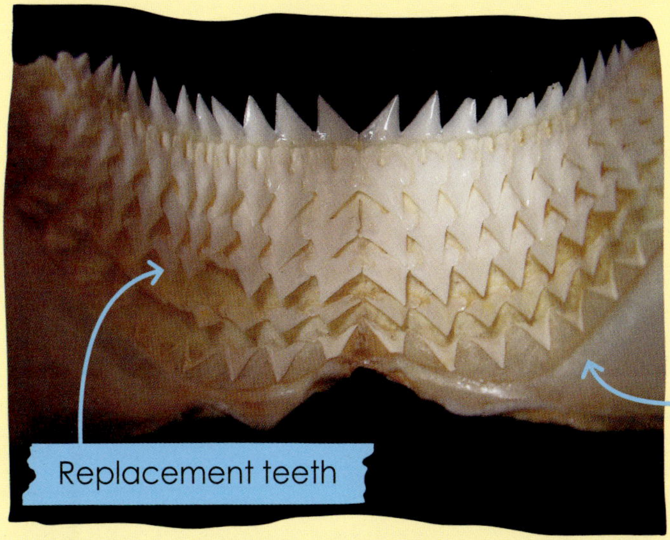

Most **species** have several rows of teeth. When teeth fall out, they are quickly replaced. Just one shark can lose thousands of teeth in its life!

THE FIERCE CREW

There are over 500 different species of shark. They are fierce animals, but only 13 species have attacked humans 10 or more times.

The fiercest sharks are:

BULL SHARK

Length: up to 11 feet (3.4 m)
Weight: up to 500 pounds (230 kg)

TIGER SHARK

Length: up to 14 feet (4.3 m)
Weight: up to 1,400 pounds (635 kg)

GREAT WHITE SHARK

Length: up to 20 feet (6.1 m)
Weight: up to 4,000 pounds (1,800 kg)

WATCH OUT FOR A GREAT WHITE SHARK'S JAWS. THIS SHARK CAN BITE WITH THREE TIMES MORE FORCE THAN A LION!

TASTE AND SPIT

Great white sharks sometimes check their prey before eating it. They want to make sure it's just right.

These sharks eat seals, which are very fatty. First, the shark bumps its prey with its snout. It does this to check how **wobbly** it is.

The shark may also take a small bite from its prey to taste it.

A rubbery diving suit will taste wrong. A hard, bony human will taste wrong too!

Great white sharks that attack people have made a mistake. They usually spit them out.

THIS HABIT IS CALLED TASTE AND SPIT.

A taste and spit attack!

READY TO HUNT

Sharks use their senses to hunt for prey and keep away from danger.

TOUCH

Sharks' skin is very **sensitive** to touch. They also have **nerves** in their teeth. Sharks bite things to explore them.

SOUND

Sharks' ears are just behind their eyes. They listen for the sounds of prey splashing.

SMELL

A great white shark can **detect** the smell of blood from about a quarter of a mile (400 m) away.

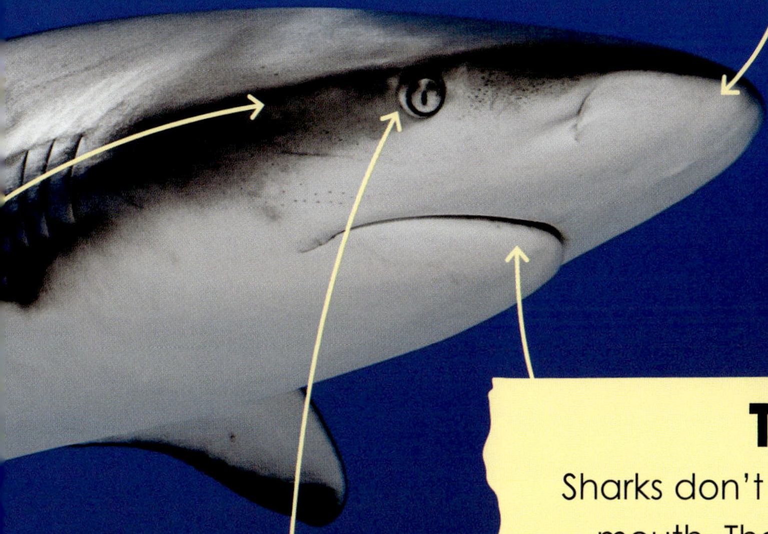

TASTE

Sharks don't just taste with their mouth. They can also taste something by rubbing up against it!

SIGHT

Sharks can see ten times better in the dark than humans can!

SUPER SENSES

Sharks have additional senses that help them get information about their environment.

ELECTRORECEPTION

Living things, including humans, produce an **electric field**. A shark's snout is covered with special **cells** that pick up on the changes in this field.

Sharks can use this sense to find a fish hiding under the sand. It can detect the fish's heartbeat!

SENSING PRESSURE CHANGES

Sharks are very good at sensing changes in pressure. They use special cells running from their snout to the tip of their tail. When a fish moves nearby, the water pressure changes. This helps the shark find its prey.

Their movements make waves that bounce off things in their environment.

Wave movements help sharks to create a 3D map of everything around them!

BREACH ATTACK

The largest great whites attack from below. They grab their prey as they burst out of the water.

The shark sees the shape of a seal at the surface. The shark swims upward at high speed with its mouth open wide. The shark bursts into the air with the seal in its mouth.

This is called a **breach** attack!

Sometimes the shark swallows the seal in one gulp as it crashes back into the water.

A lucky escape!

FEEDING FRENZY

When one shark makes a kill, the blood and splashing attract more hunters!

Soon, a crowd of sharks gathers.
The sharks kill prey as fast as possible. They feed in a **frenzy**.

Sometimes in the frenzy, sharks attack each other. Some might even take a bite out of their own tails!

Sometimes thousands of sharks gather in one place in a feeding frenzy.

ANTI-ATTACK TIPS

Shark attacks are very rare, but follow these tips just in case:

- DON'T swim in the ocean at night.
- DON'T wear sparkling jewelry in the water.
- DON'T swim when people are fishing – the struggling fish might attract sharks.
- If you get attacked, fight back! Try punching the shark in the nose.

Look out for warning signs.

KEEPING SHARKS AWAY

There are some clever inventions to protect people from sharks.

Some beaches hang a shark net out at sea. The net stops sharks from swimming too close to the shore.

Divers can wear thin **chainmail** suits. Sharks can't bite through the chainmail.

Surfers, swimmers and divers can wear a small machine strapped to one of their legs. The machine gives out electrical **pulses** that scare sharks away.

EYE-TO-EYE

Swimming with sharks is a big tourist business.

Divers are dropped into shark-infested water inside a steel cage.

A large shark is strong enough to break through the bars of the cage. However, after a quick taste of the cold metal bars, the shark will usually leave the cage alone.

Shark cages are also used by scientists. They can attach a tracking device to a shark from the safety of the cage.

Preparing for a shark encounter

Scientists track the sharks to find out how deep they dive and how far they travel each year. They also keep track of the size of shark populations, especially for **endangered** sharks.

WHO'S UNDER ATTACK?

Sharks don't attack people very often, but people can be a big danger to sharks!

Shark attacks on people are rare. Every year there are about six **unprovoked** shark attacks on people that will cause death. It may be people who are a bigger danger to sharks...

270,000 SHARKS DEAD IN ONE DAY!

Every year, about 100 million sharks are killed. That's over 270,000 per day! Most are caught as food for people. Shark meat is sold in shops and restaurants.

Some sharks die by accident. They are caught in fishing nets.

Every year, millions of sharks have their fins cut off for shark fin soup. The sharks are then thrown back into the water – still alive.

They can't swim well without their fins. So, they die because they get eaten by predators or can't swim to get enough oxygen in their body.

SHARK ALERT!

Most types of shark are now very **rare**. This includes great white sharks. Many shark species could soon become **extinct**.

WEIRD AND WONDERFUL

Not all sharks look alike. There are many different shark species around the world.

HAMMERHEAD SHARK

This shark pins stingrays to the **seafloor** using its wide head.

HORN SHARK

The horn shark sometimes uses its fins to crawl along rocks.

PORT JACKSON SHARK

Port Jackson **pups** grow in a **spiral**-shaped egg case!

WHALE SHARK

These sharks are often called "gentle giants".

HELP THE SHARKS!

- Don't eat shark fin soup or shark meat.
- Don't buy shark souvenirs, such as shark teeth and jaws.
- Don't buy belts, bags or shoes made from shark skin.
- Don't buy herbal medicines that contain shark cartilage.
- Protect sharks' **habitat** by keeping trash out of the ocean.

QUICK FACTS

LARGEST SHARK:

Whale sharks grow up to 65 feet (20 m) long

SMALLEST SHARK:

Dwarf lantern shark adults measure 6.3 – 7.9 inches (16–20 cm) long

GLOSSARY

breach – when a shark breaks the surface of the water, often jumping into the air.

cartilage – the soft tissue in the body that often supports the bone. The tip of your nose and the bottom of your ear are made of cartilage.

cell – the smallest unit of a living thing. All animals and plants are made up of cells.

chainmail – an outfit made from small metal rings connected into chains.

detect – to sense or feel something.

electric field – the area around an object where electricity is flowing.

endangered – at risk of becoming extinct (see below).

extinct – when a species of animal or plant has died out and there are none left.

fossil – a part of a dead animal or plant that has turned into rock over time.

frenzy – to behave in a wild, uncontrolled way.

habitat – the place where an animal or plant lives.

nerve – a long fiber that carries messages between body parts and the brain.

predators – animals that hunt other animals for food.

prey – an animal that is hunted by another animal as food.

pulses – short bursts of electricity.

pups – baby sharks.

rare – existing in small numbers only; not very common.

seafloor – the bottom of the sea.

sensitive – reacting or noticing more than usual.

species – a group of animals that look similar and can breed with each other.

spiral – with a continuous curved line that winds around one central point.

unprovoked – (for an attack) not caused by anything the person has said or done.

wobbly – moving from side to side easily.

INDEX

Picture credits:
(t=top; b=bottom; m=middle; l=left; r=right):
Sharkshield: 23b. Shutterstock: Alessandro De Maddelena 7bl; Le bouil baptiste 8bl; LuckyStep 1bg; Martin Prochazkacz 7t; Mark_Kostich 6b; Griffin Gillespie 8tr; Ramon Carretero 9bg; Captain Gillespie 10b, 19t; A Cotton Photo 14-15b; Damsea 15mr; Sergey Uryadnikov 16-17bg, 17tl; Martin Voeller 18-19b; BradleyvdW 20-21bg; Five Buck Photos 21tr; John Carnemolla 22b; Wildestanimal 23t; Stefan Pircher 24b; Kletr 25br; Nico Calandra 25t; VisionDive 26m; CatwalkPhotos 27m; Krzystof Odziomek 29b; BMCL 29tr; Ian Geraint Jones 29tl; Jsegalexplore 28m; Joe Belanger 28b; Nikiteev_konstantin 30bl (silhouette); Seashell World 30tr; Brandelet 2-3bg; Mapush 4-5bg; Kaschibo 12-13bg. Sipa Press/Rex Features: 11b.